Families

Table of Contents

Thematic Units

More Activities and Ideas

Reproducible Activities

Save time and energy planning thematic units with this comprehensive resource. We've searched the 1990–1998 issues of **The MAILBOX**® and **Teacher's Helper**® magazines to find the best ideas for you to use when teaching a thematic unit about families. Included in this book are favorite units from the magazines, single ideas to extend a unit, and a variety of reproducible activities. Use these activities to develop your own complete unit or simply to enhance your current lesson plans. You're sure to find everything you need for strengthening student learning.

Project Managers: Sherri Lynn Kuntz, Scott Lyons
Copy Editors: Sylvan Allen, Gina Farago, Karen Brewer Grossman, Karen L. Huffman, Amy Kirtley-Hill, Debbie Shoffner
Cover Artists: Nick Greenwood, Kimberly Richard
Artist: Jennifer L. Tipton
Typesetters: Lynette Dickerson, Mark Rainey

President, The Mailbox Book Company™: Joseph C. Bucci
Director of Book Planning and Development: Chris Poindexter
Book Development Managers: Stephen Levy, Elizabeth H. Lindsay, Thad McLaurin, Susan Walker
Curriculum Director: Karen P. Shelton
Traffic Manager: Lisa K. Pitts
Librarian: Dorothy C. McKinney
Editorial and Freelance Management: Karen A. Brudnak
Editorial Training: Irving P. Crump
Editorial Assistants: Terrie Head, Hope Rodgers, Jan E. Witcher

www.themailbox.com

Making Words. Families
am   is   ail
Sam   fail
                mail
                sail

Thematic Units...

from The MAILBOX® magazine

ALL IN THE FAMILY

There are all kinds of families: a fact that is good to keep in mind as you help your students shake the branches of their family trees to contemplate the roles, structures, traditions, rules, and sibling rivalries within.

by Lucia Kemp Henry

What It Is

What is a family anyway? Encourage students to tell about their families. Afterwards, ask students to recall the sizes, members, and customs of the families mentioned. Then sing the lyrics below to reinforce the idea that all families are unique.

(sung to the tune of "Rock-a-Bye Baby")

Families are big,
And families are small.
Families give love,
And care to us all.

People in families
Work and play, too.
I live in a family,
And so do you!

Families are different.
None are the same.
Some families have
Special names.

Families have ways,
So special and fine.
You love your family.
I sure love mine!

Family Survey

Send each student home with a copy of the survey on page 7. When all the surveys are in, graph portions of the information as a group. Give each student a photocopied school photo of himself that has been mounted on a construction paper square. Then have each student place his photo marker by the correct graph heading. Encourage students to analyze and discuss what the graph reveals. Keep the survey forms for use with several of the activities that follow.

In My Family I Have...

brother(s) only	☺	☺	
sister(s) only	☺	☺	☺
brothers and sisters	☺	☺	☺
I am an only	☺	☺	

Who Am I?

Help children learn their special roles in relation to other family members. For each student, reproduce the "Who Am I?" worksheet on page 8 and the word strips on page 9. Have students cut out the word strips. Referring to their completed surveys (page 7), have students glue appropriate role names to the space provided on "Who Am I?" Then have each student complete the worksheet picture to look like himself.

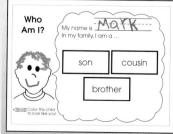

Family Flags

For each student, cut a flag shape from heavy white paper. Draw lines dividing each flag into three sections. With pencil, label each flag section with the numeral one, two, or three. In the first space, have each student draw what his family does for fun. Students may be reminded of the information on the survey, if necessary, to trigger some ideas. Have each student complete the second space with a drawing of his family working together. Students finish the flags by drawing something they love about their families in the remaining space. Mount each flag on a large sheet of construction paper, and trim to within ³/₄ inch of the white paper. On a bulletin board, display these flags with the title "We Are Family."

I'm in a Special Spot

Have students focus on their birth order and their age in relation to their siblings. (Refer to the previously completed surveys, if necessary.) For only children, have them compare their ages to those of cousins or family friends. On chart paper, have each student draw himself with his siblings (or cousins/friends). Ask him to write or dictate a sentence describing one positive aspect of his birth order.

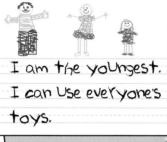

My Family Tree

Making a simple family tree is a good way for a youngster to examine his family structure. Begin by photocopying each student's school picture, and trim the copy into a circular shape. Duplicate the patterns on page 10 on light green paper. Send a copy home with each student to be filled out by a parent and returned. From the green pattern papers, have each student cut out the leaf clusters. On a 12" x 18" sheet of blue construction paper, have each student glue a brown construction paper rectangle for the tree trunk. Then have each youngster glue on six smaller strips of brown construction paper, as shown, for the tree branches. Have the student glue his picture to the tree trunk and write his name before arranging and gluing the leaf clusters as shown.

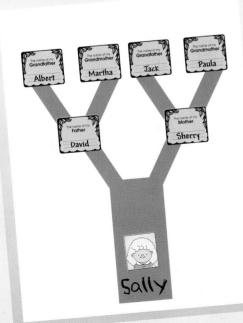

We Are Alike

You must have inherited Dad's curly hair, and Sis got her long, lanky legs from Grandpa. Your youngsters have probably heard similar comments about the origins of their looks and their interests. Have each student choose a family member with whom he shares a physical characteristic or interest. Discuss the similarities and encourage him to illustrate them on story paper. Complement the illustrations by writing student explanations of the similarities.

Birthdays in My Family

Most families have some long-standing traditions. Focus on the birthday traditions of your youngsters' families. Stimulate discussions by reading aloud *Birthday Presents* by Cynthia Rylant and asking these questions. What special things do you do when a family member has a birthday? What, if anything, do you eat that's special? How did your parents celebrate birthdays when they were little? Do you do some of the same things?

Have each student make a birthday traditions booklet. For each student, duplicate pages 11 and 12 on white or yellow construction paper. Cut the booklet pages apart, and staple them together. Then have each student write his name on the cover and draw a traditional birthday activity, a birthday food, and himself in the appropriate spaces.

My Family Rules by Scott	
A Safety Rule Look both ways before crossing street.	**A Cleanup Rule** Wipe table after eating snack.
A rule just for me Turn off computer after playing games.	**A rule I need but don't like** Bedtime is 8:30 p.m.!

Family Rules

Although a space for recording one family rule is included on the survey (page 7), you may want to assign another homework task to help students with this activity. Have each youngster discuss rules with his family. Have a parent list a family safety rule, cleanup rule, individualized rule, and one rule the child doesn't like—but understands the reasoning for. Or write the rules for the students according to their dictation. If desired, have students illustrate each of their rules.

Conflicts Are Common

From time to time, sibling conflict is certain to occur. Find out what sibling disagreements your youngsters have recently experienced. Explain that whenever people live together disagreements will eventually arise. Emphasize that we can always choose to react in a positive manner. What positive solutions have students found to recent sibling problems? Have students complete the worksheet on page 13 by finding positive solutions to common disagreements.

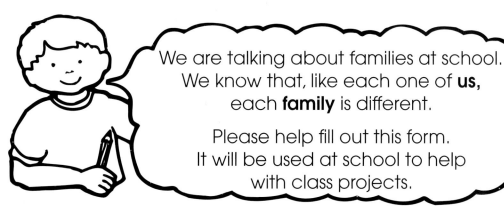

We are talking about families at school.
We know that, like each one of **us,**
each **family** is different.

Please help fill out this form.
It will be used at school to help
with class projects.

My name is _____

_____
student's name

I love my family because _____

_____

There are ☐ people in my family.
I have:

☐ sisters ☐ brothers ☐ cousins

☐ grandparents ☐ aunts ☐ uncles

I am ___ the oldest ___ the youngest ___ in the middle
___ the only child

For fun, my family likes to _____

_____

We work together on _____

_____

One of our family rules is: _____

_____

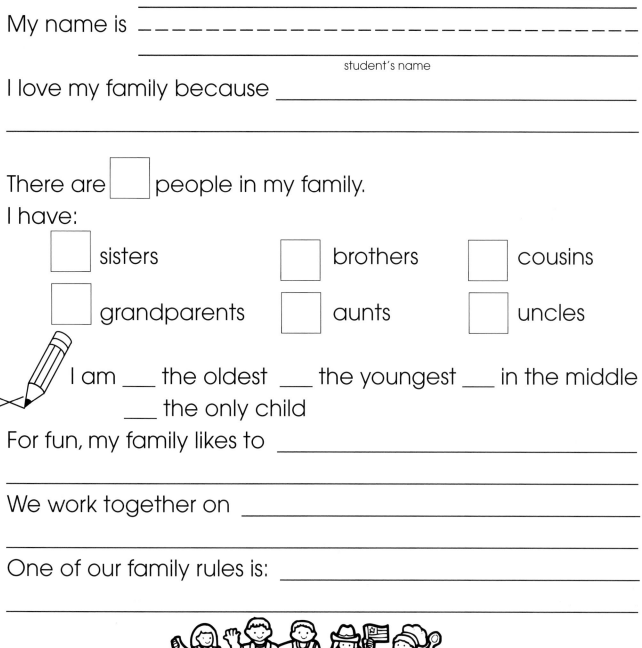

©The Education Center, Inc. • *Families* • Preschool/Kindergarten • TEC3231

Note to the teacher: Use with "Family Survey" on page 4.

7

Who Am I?

My name is _____

In my family, I am a . . .

Color this child to look like you!

Note to the teacher: Use with "Who Am I?" on page 4.

son	daughter
brother	sister
grandson	granddaughter
nephew	niece
uncle	aunt
cousin	great grandchild

Note to the teacher: Use with "Who Am I?" on page 4.

My name is _____.

Dear Parent,
We are making family trees at school.
Please help by filling out this form and returning it to school.

The name of my
Father
_____

The name of my
Mother
_____

The name of my
Grandfather
(my father's father)
_____

The name of my
Grandfather
(my mother's father)
_____

The name of my
Grandmother
(my father's mother)
_____

The name of my
Grandmother
(my mother's mother)
_____

Note to the teacher: Use with "My Family Tree" on page 5.

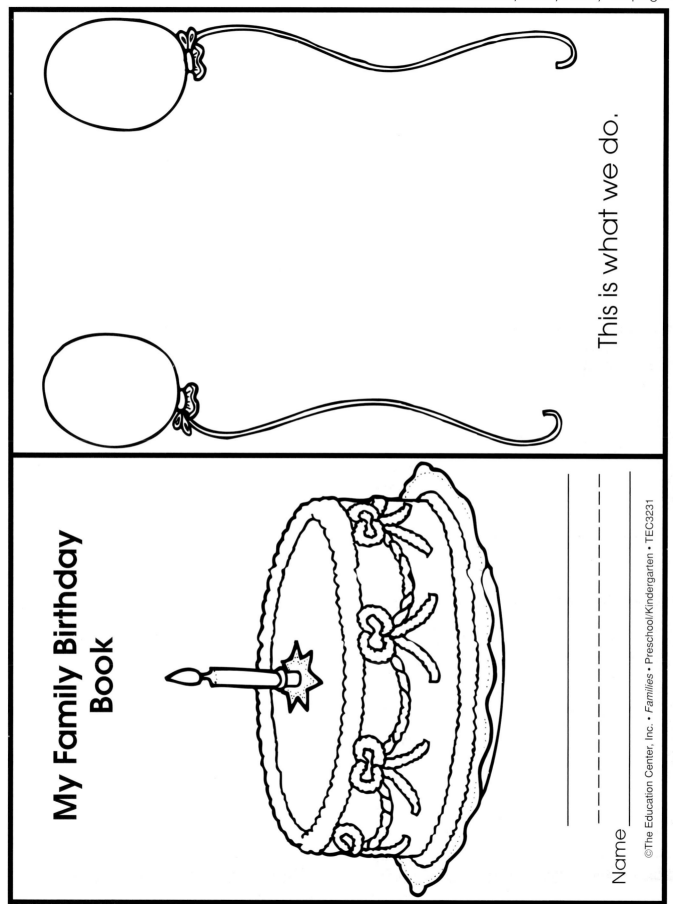

This is what we do.

My Family Birthday Book

Name

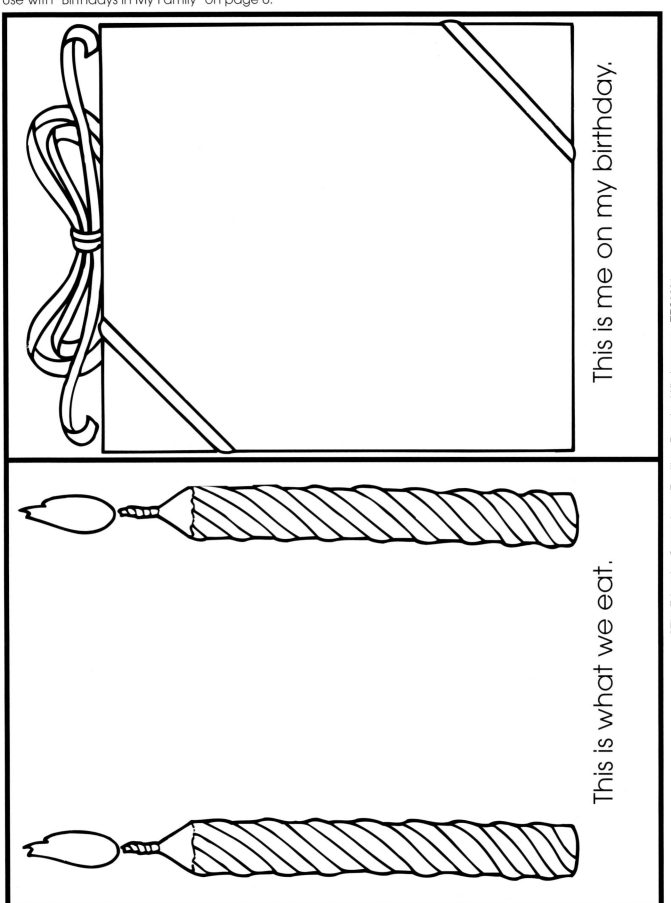

This is me on my birthday.

This is what we eat.

Getting Along
Sometimes people who love each other disagree.

Sometimes we have disagreements about:

This is what we do to get along.
✏ Draw a picture.   🖍 Color.

toys

television

chores

Note to the teacher: Use with "Conflicts Are Common" on page 6.

Home Is Where the Heart Is

Encourage parent involvement and strengthen the home-school connection with this study of families and home life. After all—learning is a family affair!

ideas by Dayle Timmons

Pictures of All in the Family

The natural way to begin a unit on families is to ask each child to share a picture of her own family. To ensure that each child has a picture to share with the class—and that the picture is one that the class can keep—purchase several disposable cameras. Send a camera home with a different child each night along with a copy of a family survey similar to the one shown. (Use the information in the surveys for projects throughout your unit.) Request that each family have a group picture taken with the camera and suggest that they discuss the survey together as an adult completes it. When every child has taken a camera home, have the pictures developed. Then prepare a lift-the-flap picture book for the class to enjoy.

For each child, cut a house shape from tagboard. Using an X-acto® knife, cut a window for peeking at the child's family picture. Glue the photo to the back of the cutout so that it is visible through the window. Glue paper hearts to the window if desired. Personalize the cutout; then laminate it. Carefully cut the window open again. Prepare a cover; then bind the pages to create a book that everyone's family will want to take a peek at!

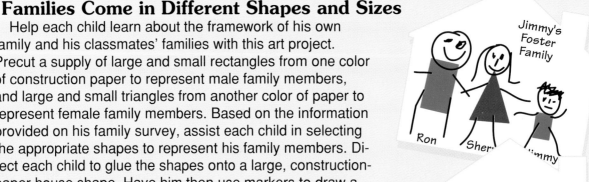

HOME Is Where the Heart Is

Johnson
Family Survey

These are our family members:
Ronnie   Dad
Rachel   Mom
Courtney   sister
Jason   brother

This is what my mommy or daddy does at home:
Daddy wakes me up

When we work together we wash the car

Courtney's Family

Families Come in Different Shapes and Sizes

Help each child learn about the framework of his own family and his classmates' families with this art project. Precut a supply of large and small rectangles from one color of construction paper to represent male family members, and large and small triangles from another color of paper to represent female family members. Based on the information provided on his family survey, assist each child in selecting the appropriate shapes to represent his family members. Direct each child to glue the shapes onto a large, construction-paper house shape. Have him then use markers to draw a head, facial features, and other body parts around each shape. Write as he dictates the names he uses to refer to each family member. When all of the projects are complete, ask small groups of children to compare the shapes of their families.

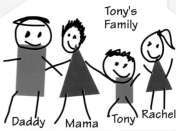

Jimmy's Foster Family

Ron   Sher   Jimmy

Tony's Family

Daddy   Mama   Tony   Rachel

Cookie-Cutter Families

Provide youngsters with sets of cookie cutters and play dough, and you'll have an opportunity to discuss family diversity. If possible obtain a Wilton® gingerbread family or nesting teddy bears cookie-cutter set (available from craft stores). Provide students with the cutters, play dough, and large house shapes cut from vinyl placemats. Encourage youngsters to use the materials to make dough representations of their own families, classmates' families, or families in familiar fairy tales and popular stories. Facilitate language development and an understanding of family by asking each child to describe her work.

Who Is in a Family?

Ask youngsters to help you name people who might be included in a family such as fathers, mothers, brothers, sisters, and grandparents. Write each suggestion on a separate sheet of bulletin-board paper. Mount the sheets of paper on a wall or low bulletin board. Then stock your art center with glue, scissors, and a supply of catalogs and magazines that include pictures of people from a variety of ethnic backgrounds. Encourage students to cut out pictures of people, and to decide what membership role each pictured person might have in a family. Then assist students in gluing their pictures to the labeled sheets that correspond with their decisions. Looks like everyone is needed in a family!

You Can Count On Families

Using the cookie-cutter sets described in "Cookie-Cutter Families," trace and cut sets of the large shape from two different colors of construction paper to represent adult male and female family members. Cut similar sets of the smaller shape to represent children. Or use shapes similar to those cut for "Families Come in Different Shapes and Sizes." Have your students create a graph to indicate the number of adults and children in each child's family. (Refer to the information given on the family surveys.) When the graph is complete, ask questions such as, "Which families have boys?", "Which families have girls?", "Who has a family with many members?", "Who has a family with only a few members?"

As a follow-up, graph fairy-tale or popular-story families. "The three pigs have a family like mine—one mommy and some boys!"

Family Graph

The Three Bears	🟢	🟤	🟡		
The Three Pigs	⚫	🟢	🟢	🟡	
Berenstain Bears	⚫	🟤	🔵	🟢	
Little Mermaid	🟡	🔵	🔵	🔵	🔵
Sleeping Beauty	🟡	⚫	🟡		

What Do Mommies and Daddies Do?

Ask your little ones this question, and out of the mouths of babes will come humorous, insightful, and simply delightful answers! Teach youngsters this chant. Then give them an opportunity to share what their daddies (or mommies) do by asking a different child each time to end the chant with his own idea such as "hug," "play ball," or "do the dishes." (If desired, refer to the responses recorded on the family surveys.) Reinforce the steady beat of the rhyme by tapping your hands on your knees.

This is what the daddies do, daddies do, daddies do.
This is what the daddies do. Daddies_____.

Supplement your discussion about the different roles mothers and fathers can have in a family with these titles. Be sure to make these and other family-related titles available for youngsters to check out and take home.

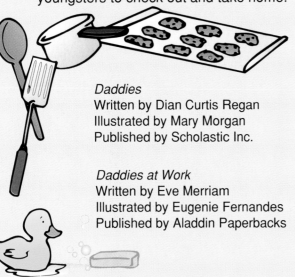

Daddies
Written by Dian Curtis Regan
Illustrated by Mary Morgan
Published by Scholastic Inc.

Daddies at Work
Written by Eve Merriam
Illustrated by Eugenie Fernandes
Published by Aladdin Paperbacks

Mommies
Written by Dian Curtis Regan
Illustrated by Mary Morgan
Published by Scholastic Inc.

Mommies at Work
Written by Eve Merriam
Illustrated by Eugenie Fernandes
Published by Aladdin Paperbacks

Role-Play Day

Now that youngsters have a better understanding of the roles mothers and fathers can have in a family, why not have a role-play day? Ask parents to allow children to wear articles of adult clothing over the children's regular school clothing on the day designated as role-play day. Prior to the day, for each child personalize a bag for the storage of the adult clothing items so that if desired, the children may take off the adult items during the day. During a morning group time, ask volunteers to pantomime some of the jobs that their parents do at home such as feeding a baby, cutting the grass, or cooking dinner. By pretending to do some of the things that moms and dads do for their families, youngsters will gain a better understanding of how families share household responsibilities.

Family Ties

Use these literature links as you discuss the diversity in families and home life. If necessary, paraphrase the text or discuss the illustrations to meet students' interest levels.

Families
Written by Meredith Tax
Illustrated by Marylin Hafner
Published by Little, Brown and Company

All Kinds of Families
Written by Norma Simon
Illustrated by Joe Lasker
Published by Albert Whitman & Company

Homespun Family Fun

Fun-filled family projects that every member of the family will enjoy!

Families Work and Play Together

If you'll be sending a family survey home (see "Pictures of All in the Family"), you might want to ask families to include brief descriptions of how they work and how they play together. Write each child's responses on sentence strips; then mount the statements on a bulletin board. Send an empty envelope home with each child. Request that each family look through catalogs and magazines for pictures of families working or playing together. Ask that they cut the pictures out and return them to school in the envelope. Assist each child in mounting her collected pictures on the board among the children's statements.

Homestyle Homework

Provide each child with a large sheet of art paper, rolled up and ready to take home. Send along a note requesting that each family cut and decorate the paper to resemble their abode—whether it be an apartment building, mobile home, or house. Mount a construction-paper road to a bulletin board along with the title "Home Is Where the Heart Is." Display the returned projects on the board along with pictures of the students' families.

Fine-Feathered Families

This turkey beams with family pride! Mount a large turkey character onto a wall or bulletin board. Send a large, brightly colored, paper feather home with each child along with a note encouraging his family to embellish the feather as desired. When the feathers are returned, display them around the turkey to create a fine-feathered fowl.

Laleña Williams—Special Needs Preschoolers
St. Francis Preschool—LaGrange Site
LaGrangeville, NY

Preschool Pumpkin Patch

Combine a surprise preschool pumpkin patch with a family picnic. Announce the date of a class picnic and pumpkin hunt to parents. Keeping the patch a secret from youngsters, ask parents to donate small pumpkins to your class. Before youngsters arrive at school on the morning of the picnic, arrange the pumpkins in an open area of your school's playground. Enjoy a day of pumpkin picking and picnicking!

adapted from an idea by Linda N. Roth—
   Four- and Five-Year-Olds
First Step Preschool
Black Forest, CO

Siblings Are Sensational!

Looking for ideas that your little ones can relate to? Oh boy! Here's a collection for you. Whether each child in your class is a big brother or sister, a little brother or sister, or an only child, these activities will help him or her understand and share common family experiences. Use the activities on pages 20–21 to honor youngsters who become new big brothers or sisters.

ideas by dayle timmons

The Scoop on Siblings

Since young preschoolers might have a difficult time articulating the ages and names of their siblings, contact parents to make sure you have accurate information. Duplicate a class supply of a parent note such as the one shown; then send them home. Soon you'll have information about every child and his brother—and sister!

Dear Parent,

We are learning what it's like to be a big brother or sister, a little brother or sister, or an only child. Please make sure we have the correct information.

My child's name _____.

His/her brothers' names and ages:

_____

His/her sisters' names and ages:

_____

If you are expecting a baby, when is it due?

_____

Thank you,
Mrs. Timmons

How Many Brothers? How Many Sisters?

Sibling relationships can be puzzling, but all the pieces fit together nicely with these visual helps. Using the information from the returned parent notes (see "The Scoop on Siblings"), collect enough cardboard puzzle pieces (that resemble people shapes) so that you have one for each child and his or her correct number of siblings. To prepare, spray-paint the appropriate number of pieces one color to represent sisters and the remaining pieces a different color to represent brothers. When the paint is dry, use a black marker to add dot eyes to each piece. Have each child choose the pieces that represent the children in his family—a piece for himself and one for each of his siblings. Then have him glue the pieces on an index card. Write the siblings' names by the pieces.

During a group time, have the class look at each child's card as he tells about the children in his family. Spread the cards out in front of the group. Ask questions to help the children find similarities and differences. Which families have two brothers? Which families have three children? Are the numbers of brothers and sisters the same in those families? Which families have only one child? Finally, graph the cards by the number of children in each family.

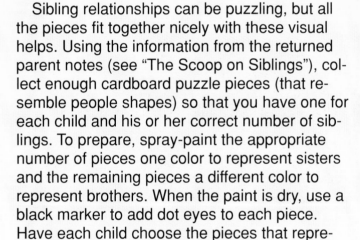

Ben   Beth

A Salute to Siblings

This song invites youngsters to stand up for "sibling-hood." Hooray!

(sung to the tune of "If You're Happy and You Know It")

If you have a big [brother/sister], stand right up.
If you have a big [brother/sister], stand right up.
Big [brothers/sisters], it's true, are older than you.
If you have a big [brother/sister], stand right up.

If you have a little [brother/sister], stand right up.
If you have a little [brother/sister], stand right up.
Little [brothers/sisters], it's true, are younger than you.
If you have a little [brother/sister], stand right up.

If you're an only child, stand right up.
If you're an only child, stand right up.
In your own family, you are special—yes sirree!
If you're an only child, stand right up.

Super Siblings

Perhaps your little ones are so proud of their siblings that they want to show them off! If so, prepare a bulletin board titled "Super Siblings." Encourage students to display photos and illustrations on the board. Invite children without siblings to draw pictures of their friends with their siblings. Also invite children to cut out magazine pictures that show children who could be siblings; then help them attach these pictures to the board.

Bodacious Brothers and Super Sisters

Now that you know who has brothers and sisters, find out what your children think about them. On each of three different colors of bulletin-board paper, draw the outline shape of a child. Cut out these shapes; then label each one with one of the following phrases: "Big Brother or Sister," "Little Brother or Sister," and "Only Child." Display the cutouts on a wall. During a group time, ask volunteers to tell about children's big brothers or sisters or share stories about them. On the appropriate cutout, write the children's descriptions and one-sentence summaries. During another group time, similarly discuss little brothers and sisters. Next give only children a chance to share. Help children see the similarities and differences in their situations.

Sibling Stories

Since most of your children with brothers and sisters have probably had at least one good case of "sibling-itis," the situations in these stories will be familiar ones.

Geraldine First
Written & Illustrated by Holly Keller
Published by Greenwillow Books

I Love You the Purplest
Written by Barbara M. Joosse
Illustrated by Mary Whyte
Published by Chronicle Books

Bunny Cakes
Written & Illustrated by Rosemary Wells
Published by Dial Books For Young Readers

Ben and his sister.

Congratulations!

Chances are that one or more of your preschoolers will welcome the arrival of a new baby into her family. Honor the proud, new brother or sister with a crown and certificate. Duplicate the crown (page 22) and the certificate (page 23) onto construction paper; then cut them out. Color both items, if desired. Personalize the crown as shown; then tape a matching construction-paper strip to the crown so that it fits the child's head. Program the certificate; then mount it onto a larger piece of paper. Present the crown and certificate to the proud sibling during a group time; then invite her to tell about the most important baby in the world—her new brother or sister!

Nancy Goldberg—Three-Year-Olds, B'nai Israel Nursery School
Rockville, MD

Brothers and Sisters in Training

Set up a dramatic-play center that resembles a nursery so that the big brothers and sisters in your class can train their classmates in their new area of expertise. In addition to baby dolls, place items in the center such as empty baby-powder containers, bibs, empty baby-food containers (avoid glass jars), bottles, diapers, a lullaby cassette, and a rocking chair. My, what big helpers you all are!

"Rocka-My-Baby"

Every big brother and sister is sure to need to know how to rock a baby to sleep. Have youngsters share familiar lullabies that they already know, such as "Hush, Little Baby" and "Rock-a-Bye, Baby." Then continue your sibling training with this simple, but sweet, song.

(sung to the tune of "Mary Had a Little Lamb")

Hush, lil' baby, time to sleep,
Time to sleep, time to sleep.
Hush, lil' baby, time to sleep.
Rest quietly.

Hush, lil' baby, [brother/sister] loves you.
[Brother/sister] loves you. [Brother/sister] loves you.
Hush, lil' baby, [brother/sister] loves you.
Rest quietly.

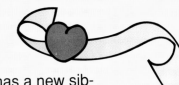

Books for the Big Brother or Sister

Books abound for the child who is new in "sibling-hood." When a child has a new sibling, read aloud one of the following titles during storytime. Consider also preparing this thoughtful gift for the child to take home. Label a diaper bag "For Big Brothers and Big Sisters." Fill the bag with several of the following titles. Also include a note to the parents congratulating them on their new arrival, and encouraging them to use the books to spark discussion with their preschooler about the changes ahead. When the diaper bag is returned, record several words of advice from the child about taking care of a baby brother or sister. Put this advice in the bag before passing it to the next child.

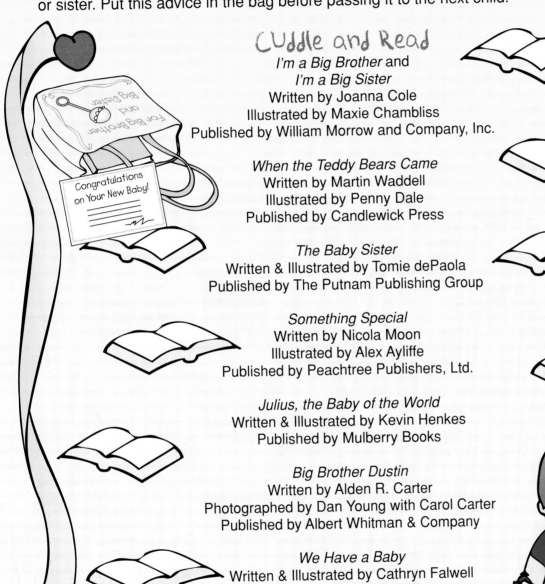

Cuddle and Read

I'm a Big Brother and
I'm a Big Sister
Written by Joanna Cole
Illustrated by Maxie Chambliss
Published by William Morrow and Company, Inc.

When the Teddy Bears Came
Written by Martin Waddell
Illustrated by Penny Dale
Published by Candlewick Press

The Baby Sister
Written & Illustrated by Tomie dePaola
Published by The Putnam Publishing Group

Something Special
Written by Nicola Moon
Illustrated by Alex Ayliffe
Published by Peachtree Publishers, Ltd.

Julius, the Baby of the World
Written & Illustrated by Kevin Henkes
Published by Mulberry Books

Big Brother Dustin
Written by Alden R. Carter
Photographed by Dan Young with Carol Carter
Published by Albert Whitman & Company

We Have a Baby
Written & Illustrated by Cathryn Falwell
Published by Clarion Books

The New Baby: A Mister Rogers' Neighborhood®
First Experiences Book
Written by Fred Rogers
Photographed by Jim Judkis
Published by PaperStar

Ellen and Penguin and the New Baby
Written & Illustrated by Clara Vulliamy
Published by Candlewick Press

Crown

Use with "Congratulations!" on page 20.

Sibling Certificate

This is to certify that

_____
child's name

is qualified to be a big _____
brother or sister

Congratulations on the arrival of

_____
baby's name

born on _____
birthdate

We are very happy to share this occasion!

_____
teachers' names

©The Education Center, Inc. • *Families* • Preschool/Kindergarten • TEC3231

Families Are Fun!

We all know that families come in many different packages. In fact, no two are exactly the same! Introduce your students to the topic of families with these fun ideas.

by Sherri Lynn Kuntz and Angela VanBeveren

What is a family?
- people who love each other
  —Keisha
- A family is people you live with.
  —Brit
- they hug a lot
  —Camille

Getting Started

Begin your family unit by having youngsters respond to the question, "What is a family?" You are sure to get many different answers! Record each student's response on a sheet of chart paper. Then introduce some general information about families (see illustration below). Also record what students would like to learn about families. Display the chart for future reference and encourage students to add to it throughout the unit.

Families Are Special!

Use a familiar tune to get your youngsters in sync with families! During group time, sing the song below with your students. After the children know the song well, encourage them to come up with motions for each line. Are families special? Of course!

(sung to the tune of "Ten Little Indians")

Some have fathers. Some have mothers.
Some have sisters. Some have brothers.
In some houses, there are others.
Every family's special!

Facts About Families!
A family is made up of a group of people who live together.
Family members protect, nurture, teach, and provide for each other.
Sometimes family members look alike and sometimes they do not.
Every person in a family helps make it special.
Families are alike in some ways and different in other ways.
Families can be large or small.
Other people sometimes live with a family.

Aren't They Great?

Show your students that families are bunches of fun with this listening activity. In advance, cut out a white poster board circle for each child. Instruct each student to use a permanent marker to draw a smiley face on her circle. Then have her use crayons to color the entire face. To complete the prop, have her tape a craft stick to the back of the face. Then gather your little ones and ask them questions such as, "Does your family ever watch movies?" and "Does your family eat ice cream together?" Have students answer yes to questions by holding up their smiley-face props. Once youngsters get the idea, encourage them to take turns asking questions. Your youngsters will be all smiles as they realize that their families do many of the same fun things!

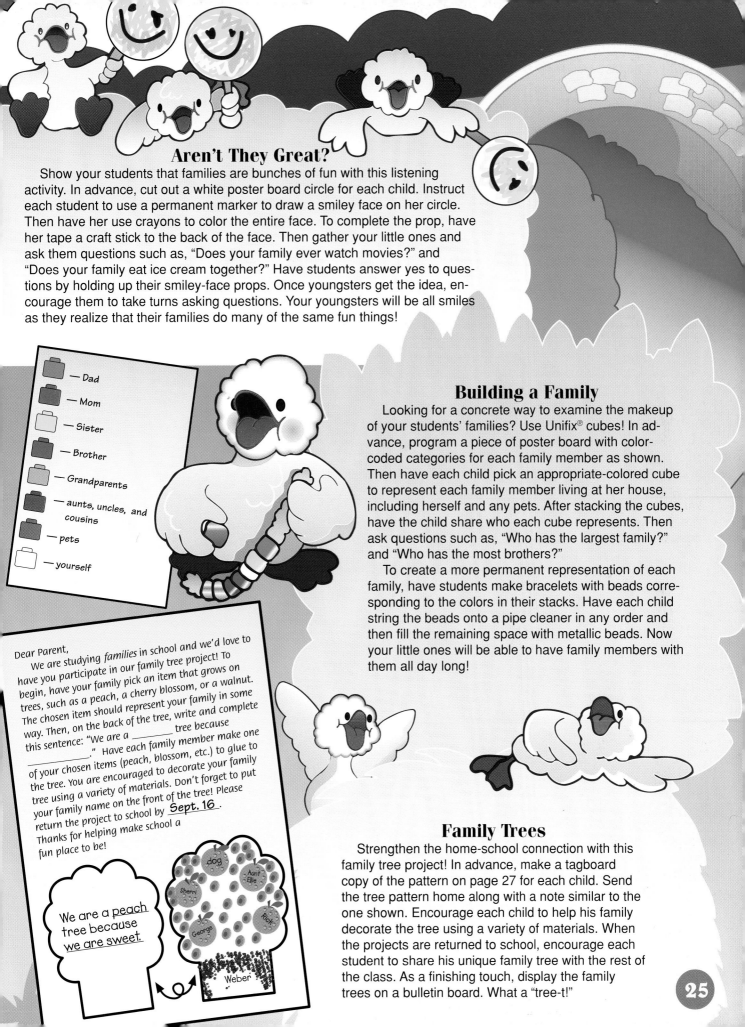

— Dad
— Mom
— Sister
— Brother
— Grandparents
— aunts, uncles, and cousins
— pets
— yourself

Building a Family

Looking for a concrete way to examine the makeup of your students' families? Use Unifix® cubes! In advance, program a piece of poster board with color-coded categories for each family member as shown. Then have each child pick an appropriate-colored cube to represent each family member living at her house, including herself and any pets. After stacking the cubes, have the child share who each cube represents. Then ask questions such as, "Who has the largest family?" and "Who has the most brothers?"

To create a more permanent representation of each family, have students make bracelets with beads corresponding to the colors in their stacks. Have each child string the beads onto a pipe cleaner in any order and then fill the remaining space with metallic beads. Now your little ones will be able to have family members with them all day long!

Dear Parent,
We are studying *families* in school and we'd love to have you participate in our family tree project! To begin, have your family pick an item that grows on trees, such as a peach, a cherry blossom, or a walnut. The chosen item should represent your family in some way. Then, on the back of the tree, write and complete this sentence: "We are a _____ tree because _____." Have each family member make one of your chosen items (peach, blossom, etc.) to glue to the tree. You are encouraged to decorate your family tree using a variety of materials. Don't forget to put your family name on the front of the tree! Please return the project to school by **Sept. 16**. Thanks for helping make school a fun place to be!

We are a peach tree because we are sweet.

dog
Aunt Ellie
Sherri
George
Rick
Weber

Family Trees

Strengthen the home-school connection with this family tree project! In advance, make a tagboard copy of the pattern on page 27 for each child. Send the tree pattern home along with a note similar to the one shown. Encourage each child to help his family decorate the tree using a variety of materials. When the projects are returned to school, encourage each student to share his unique family tree with the rest of the class. As a finishing touch, display the family trees on a bulletin board. What a "tree-t!"

What Children Do Best

As we all know, every member of a family is important! This art activity will help each child understand his significance in his family. Read *What Mommies Do Best/What Daddies Do Best* by Laura Numeroff. After discussing the book, have students brainstorm other things that parents do. Record responses on a piece of chart paper. Then ask each child to think of one thing that he does best and have him draw a picture of the activity on a sheet of construction paper. Label students' drawings and then display them on a bulletin board with the title "What Children Do Best!" If desired, include a modified phrase similar to the one from the book's ending. What a masterpiece!

School Families Are Sweet!

Culminate your family unit with this yummy circle game that extends the idea of a family to the classroom setting. Explain that classroom members are a special type of family. Review "Facts About Families!" on page 24 and discuss how they relate to school. To play the game, chant the rhyme below with your students while passing around a piece of wrapped candy. When the rhyme has ended, have the student with the piece of candy share something positive about a school friend. Then have her give the candy to the child next to her and move to the middle of the circle. When all of your sweeties are in the middle, encourage a group hug. Then give each student a piece of candy to munch on. Now that's a wonderfully sweet ending!

We are sweet.
We are neat!
We are a family.
What a treat!

Read All About Families!

The Berenstain Bears Are a Family
Written by Stan and Jan Berenstain
Published by Random House, Inc.

Me and My Family Tree
Written by Joan Sweeney
Published by Crown Publishers, Inc.

Geraldine's Baby Brother
Written by Holly Keller
Published by Greenwillow Books

One Hundred Is a Family
Written by Pam Muñoz Ryan
Published by Hyperion Books for Children

Will You Take Care of Me?
Written by Margaret Park Bridges
Published by Morrow Junior Books

The Baby Sister
Written by Tomie dePaola
Published by G. P. Putnam's Sons

Louanne Pig in the Perfect Family
Written by Nancy L. Carlson
Published by Carolrhoda Books, Inc.

Octopus Hug
Written by Laurence Pringle
Published by Boyds Mills Press, Inc.

Horace
Written by Holly Keller
Published by Mulberry Books

The _____

Family Tree

Kindred Ideas

Watch Your Garden Grow

Here's a display idea that promotes the home-school connection and decorates your hallway! At the beginning of the year, line your hallway with a white picket fence (wooden or poster board). Cut out vine and leaf shapes from bulletin-board paper, and mount them on the fence. At the beginning of each month, send home a seasonal tagboard shape (see box for suggestions) for students and parents to jointly decorate. After students share their family projects with the class, mount them behind the fence.

Margaret Power, Mary Markos, Jerry
    Pavelka, and Lois Schultz—Gr. K
Wood River Elementary
Corpus Christi, TX

Sept.	apples
Oct.	pumpkins
Nov.	turkeys
Dec.	gifts
Jan.	snowpeople
Feb.	hearts
Mar.	kites or eggs
Apr.	eggs or umbrellas
May	flowers
June	suns

Family Portraits

"House" this for a fun families project? For each child, cut a simple house shape from the middle of a sheet of colored construction paper. Have each child glue the resulting outline to a sheet of white construction paper. Then provide crayons or markers, and have each child draw her family members and pets inside her house shape.

Tammy Bruhn—PreK
Temperance, MI

A "Work" Book

Children are proud to talk about their parents and their understanding of what they do at work. Create a class book about jobs by requesting that one parent or caregiver for each child write a brief description of his or her occupation. Copy each description on construction paper; then ask each child to illustrate her parent's job description. Bind the pages between covers; then read the book aloud. This project is sure to do a good job of involving parents!

Mary E. Maurer, Caddo, OK

I work at a publishing company as an in-house artist. I draw all day and get paid for it.
Mr. Crane

I work at home taking care of Susie's little brother.
Mrs. Young

These Families Love Books

Here's a great display that encourages reading at school *and* at home. Simply send home a disposable camera along with a note requesting that a parent take a photo of his child reading a favorite book with another family member. Have the film developed; then tape each picture behind a child-decorated construction-paper frame. Mount the framed photos along with a border of colorful book jackets on a bulletin board. Title the board "These Families Love Books!"

adapted from an idea by
   Andrea Esposito—Preschool
VA/YMCA Child Care Center
Brooklyn, NY

Sibling Celebrations

A baby shower for a kindergartner? Why not? The arrival of a new family member is the perfect time to hold a special celebration to boost a sibling-in-waiting's pride and ease his anxiety. To prepare, have each child in the class sign a paper bag; then fill the bag with baby items, such as a rattle, booties, and sample-sized baby products. During the event, invite the proud sibling to wear a paper banner labeled with "It's a girl [or boy]!" Serve refreshments to the class and give lots of congratulatory attention to the child. Then present the child with the bag of baby goods to take home.

Elesa Miller—Gr. K
St. Catherine Laboure
Wheaton, MD

Tommy
Heather
Lisa
Jimmy
George
Kenneth
Mike
Alice
Donna

Oh, when my mom tucks me in bed...

When I was young...
I liked riding a bicycle.

by Ian's dad

Oh, When My Mom...

Moms and children will all feel special when you sing this Mother's Day song. Each time you repeat the song, ask a different child to supply a phrase to fill in the blank.

(sung to the tune of "When the Saints Go Marching In")

Oh, when my mom [gives me a hug],
Oh, when my mom [gives me a hug],
Oh, I know that I am special,
When my mom [gives me a hug].

Trish Draper—Gr. K, Millarville Community School
Millarville, Alberta, Canada

Getting Parents Into Kids' Books

Entice parents and other family members into sharing their writing and illustrating abilities with your class. *When I Was Young in the Mountains* by Cynthia Rylant is one book that lends itself nicely to this activity. After sharing the book with your class, have each child dictate and illustrate a page of his own by completing the sentence "When I was young...." Assemble all of the pages into a book with a pocket for the original book and a blank page behind each child's page. Give each child a turn to take the book home and have a family member write and illustrate the page behind his page. Everyone eagerly awaits each new addition.

Bev Wirt, Desert Valley School, Glendale, AZ

Here's a display that will go perfectly with your unit about families. Ask each child's family to attach photos of family members to a personalized sheet of construction paper. Mount the collected sheets together on a wall to resemble a quilt; then add a border. Invite parents to take a good look at your display of classy families.

Penny Horne—Preschool
University of Maine at Presque Isle
  Daycare
Presque Isle, ME

The House That Jack Built

Youngsters can create original booklets using this familiar story pattern. For each child, duplicate copies of four different pages, each containing one of the following open sentences: *This is _____.* *This is the house that _____ built. This is the family that lives in the house that _____ built. These are the pets that live with the family that lives in the house that _____ built.* Have each youngster fill in his name on each page and illustrate it. Then have him glue construction paper cutouts atop the sheets of construction paper to resemble the front and back of a house. To complete each booklet, add the title to each youngster's front cover; then staple his completed pages between the construction paper covers.

Sara McCormick Davis—Gr. K, Wiley Post Elementary
Oklahoma City, OK

Family Ties

Focus on families with this "tie-riffic" display. Cut out a class supply of necktie shapes from wallpaper samples. Ask each parent to help his child find a family photo to bring to school. Invite each child to share her photo and name the family members in the picture. Then attach each photo to a wallpaper necktie, label the tie with the child's name, and display these family ties on a door or bulletin board. We are family!

Kristy Curless—Infants
Chesterbrook Academy
Champaign, IL

The Family Tree

Invite your children's families to help you keep this year-round display decorated. Mount a large paper tree in a hallway or on a bulletin board near your school's entrance. Every month, provide each child's family with a seasonal construction-paper shape to creatively decorate. Arrange these projects on the tree's branches. Look what's on the family tree this month!

Suzi Dodson—Preschool
Growing Years Early Learning Center
Claysburg, PA

Now You're a Big Brother/Sister!

Boost the wavering self-esteem of your little ones when they become big brothers and sisters. Right before a child has a new arrival in her home, prepare a large card that says "_____ will be a great big _____ because…" On the inside of the card, have the other children dictate why they think that child will be a good big sister. Then invite each child to provide an illustration on the card and sign it. When the new baby arrives, give the older sibling her card and invite her to read it to the class.

Linda LaPlume—Gr. K, St. Matthew School of the Arts, Cranston, RI

Tamika will make a **GREAT** big sister because…

Reproducible Activities...

Note to the Teacher

While teaching this unit on families, be very much aware to include all kinds of families in society today. You may want to survey the family compositions evident in your classroom to make sure those particular families are discussed and respected. This unit features step families, families with handicapped members, family celebrations, and family member titles or names. As you discuss and complete each worksheet with your class, allow ample time for sharing and open discussion about families. It will be important to emphasize the concepts of interdependence, caring, and love more than those members who actually constitute "family."

Oral Instructions for Page 35

1. Each family lives in a home. Just as each family is different, so are the homes in which they live.
2. Look at the pictures of the homes on this sheet and identify the home most like the one in which you live. Color the home.
3. Now, in the middle of the sheet, in the big empty box, you should draw a picture of your family. A family is what makes the place you live a home.
4. Draw a line from the picture of your family to the picture of your home.

Extension Activities Families

If there are instances of "special" families in your classroom (such as a step family, grandparent who is the primary caregiver, handicapped member, adopted children), invite them to speak to your children.

Set up a book corner with a variety of books that feature different family situations.

Grandfather and I by Helen Buckley (Lothrop, Lee and Shepard, 1961)
Grandmother and I by Helen Buckley (Lothrop, Lee and Shepard, 1961)

Name _____

Our Home

My family lives here.

✏️ Draw your family in the box.

✏️ Draw a line from your family to a home like yours.

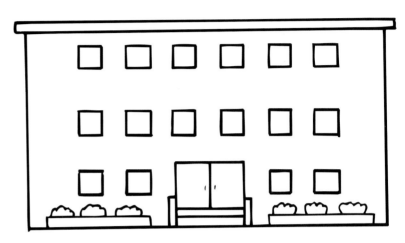

Oral Instructions for Page 37

1. All families are special and each one is different.
2. This worksheet shows a picture of a special family called a "step family."
3. The father has two children by him in this picture, but the mother in the picture is not their mother. She is their stepmother. The mother has two other children by her in the picture, but the father in the picture is not their father. He is their stepfather.
4. A step family is like two families put together. When this happens, the children will have a stepfather or stepmother or stepbrothers and stepsisters too!
5. A step family is very special. Like any family, there can be much love and caring in a step family.
6. In this step family, there are two brothers and two sisters. How many brothers and sisters do you have? Write the numerals in the boxes at the bottom of the sheet.

A Family

Together they make a family.

I have ☐ brothers and ☐ sisters.

Oral Instructions for Page 39

1. What is this family doing?
2. How are they helping each other?
3. What is special about the mother?
4. How does she help her family? This mother can do many things for her family. Her wheelchair helps her get from place to place.
5. How does her family help her?
6. How do you help your family? *(Help the children write or dictate a sentence completion to finish "I help my family _____.")*

Name _____

Working Together

Families help each other.

I help my family _____

Oral Instructions for Page 41

1. We usually do not live with all the people in our whole family. There are other family members that are special to us. They have special names.

2. Help me think of some of these special names. *(Pause.)* That's right, we have moms, dads, grandparents, aunts, uncles, cousins. *(Add as many special names as the children named.)*

3. Find the child on your sheet. Color her. The picture shows many people in the child's whole family. Find the child's parents and color them. Find the child's aunts and uncles. Aunts and uncles are your parents' sisters and brothers. Color the aunts and uncles. Find the child's grandparents. Grandparents are your parents' mothers and fathers. Color the grandparents.

4. At the bottom of your sheet are some special family names for you to match. Cut out the name boxes at the bottom and match them to the name boxes by the correct pictures of the family members.

A Family Portrait

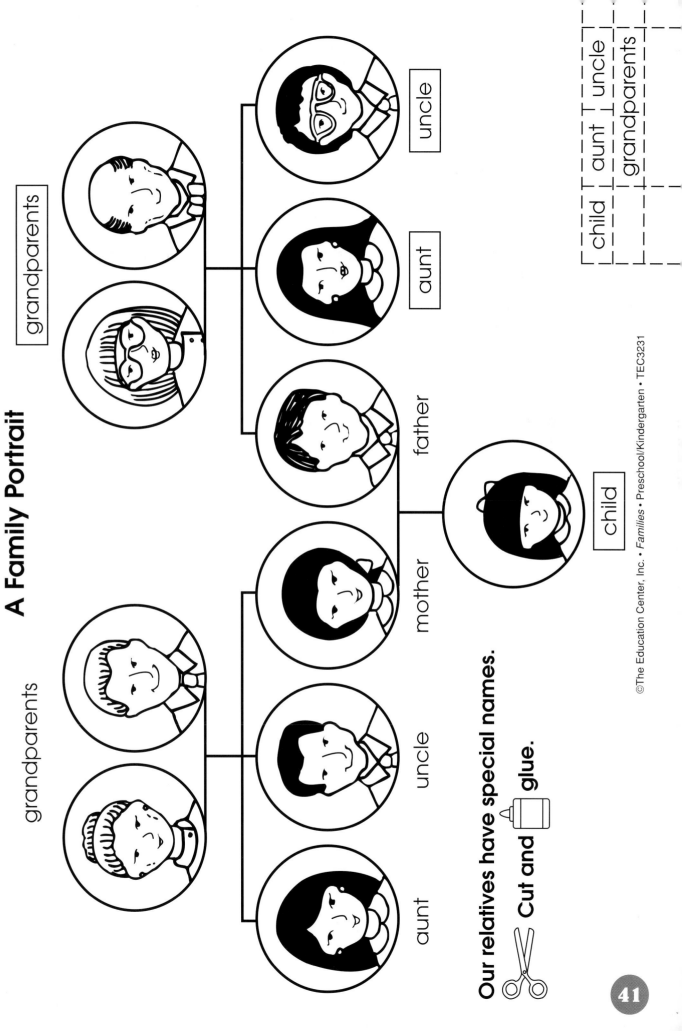

grandparents

grandparents

uncle

aunt

father

mother

aunt

uncle

child

Our relatives have special names.

Cut and glue.

child	aunt	uncle
	grandparents	

Oral Instructions for Page 43

1. Families celebrate special days together.
2. Look at the first picture. This is a boy and his grandmother. She is teaching him about a special family holiday. Does anyone know what holiday it is? That's right, the holiday is called Hanukkah. What holidays does your family celebrate? Trace the words below this picture about Hanukkah. The words say "a holiday."
3. Look at the next picture. This is a girl and her father. They share special family times together. They like to visit the zoo and buy ice cream for a treat. What special times do you enjoy with your family? Trace the words below the picture. The words say "a treat."
4. The next family is having a party. They are playing a special game. They are trying to hit the piñata. The piñata is filled with toys and treats. What special activities or customs does your family enjoy at a party? Trace the words below the picture. The words say "a party."
5. Look at the last picture. This family is celebrating a special day. They have a cake and presents. What are they celebrating? How does your family celebrate birthdays? Trace the words below the picture. The words say "a birthday."

Special Days

Each family has its own special ways.

✏️ Trace.

🖍️ Color.

1. a holiday

2. a treat

3. a party

4. a birthday

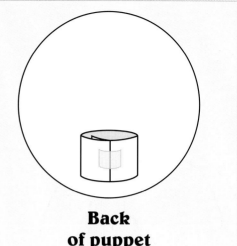

Back of puppet

How to Use Page 45

Duplicate the puppets on heavy paper for durability.

Have children color the faces, then cut them out. After they cut out the six paper rings, size rings to fit their fingers and paste. Glue a ring at the bottom of the back side of each face. The ring at the bottom allows children to bend their fingers.

When finished, encourage role-playing. Have children work together to combine puppet "families." You may want to tape-record children's plays to stimulate class discussion later.

Extension Activities

- Discuss the differences and likenesses in each other's appearances—eye color, hair, height, etc. Talk about things and situations that make your students happy, sad, and afraid. Give each child the opportunity to talk about his favorite toy and food.
- Make "Me" booklets. Staple four sheets of paper together for each student. Write a "feeling word" (angry, lonely, happy, excited) at the top of each page. Students draw or cut out and paste pictures on that page of things that make them feel that way.
- Cover a box with bright paper and magazine pictures of animals. Cut a hole in the box large enough for your hand. Give each child an animal cutout. Help each child write two or three words on his animal that will identify him (a physical trait, favorite color, or family member). Place all cutouts in the box. Each day, pull out three animals and read aloud the information on them. Children try to guess who the animals are. After guessing, let the children to whom the animals belong hang them on a bulletin board. Continue until the box is empty.
- Discuss the differences and likenesses of your students' homes and families. For each child, fold a large piece of white paper in half. Have students draw their house on one side. Help them cut out a door and windows to see inside. Provide magazines and scissors. Students cut out and glue inside the houses pictures of people to represent their families' members. The family will show through the door and windows.
- With your class, list three or four ways they can feel inside. Ask different students to take turns showing how their faces look if they feel like the words on the list. Have them use their whole bodies to show how they feel. Have the class take turns making sounds (no words allowed) that represent the words on the list.
- Make "Personality Pillows" for children to use at naptime. Give each child two 12-inch squares of preshrunk muslin. Have each child use permanent markers to write their name and draw three of their favorite things on one of their squares. Sew the two squares together except for a small opening, stuff with nylons or scrap material, and finish sewing.

Family Talk

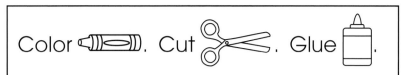

Paper ring patterns

Like Father, Like Son

Make the son look just like his father.

Grandma's Cookies
Draw in the chips for each cookie.

Name _____

Family Photo Album

Look at the pictures from left to right. Draw an X on the picture in each row that does not belong.